Ocean City, N.J.
An Illustrated History

Susan K. Miller

Dedication

To my husband, Fred—if I hadn't met you on the beach, I wouldn't be living here in paradise now!

Acknowledgments

I would like to thank my husband, Fred, for his knowledge, encouragement, and hard work in helping me organize and write this book; Stu Sirott for his technical know-how and hard work; and my sister and brother-in-law, Joan and Allan Okin, for their help. I also want to thank the Ocean City Historical Museum, Don Doll, and Dawn Brown for loaning postcards from their collections for use in this book.

Other Schiffer Books on Related Subjects
The Ocean City Boardwalk, by Dean Davis
Touring New Jersey's Lighthouses, by Mary Beth Temple and Patricia Wylupek
Cape May Point: The Illustrated History from 1875 to the Present, by Joe Jordan
Cape May Point: Three Walking Tours of Historic Cottages, by Joe Jordan

Copyright © 2007 by Susan K. Miller
Library of Congress Control Number: 2007924597

Covers and book designed by: Bruce Waters
Type set in Aldine 721 BT and headings Huminest 521 Ubd

ISBN: 978-0-7643-2709-4
Printed in China

Published by Schiffer Publishing Ltd.
4880 Lower Valley Road
Atglen, PA 19310
Phone: (610) 593-1777; Fax: (610) 593-2002
E-mail: Info@schifferbooks.com

For the largest selection of fine reference books on this and related subjects, please visit our web site at **www.schifferbooks.com**
We are always looking for people to write books on new and related subjects. If you have an idea for a book please contact us at the above address.

This book may be purchased from the publisher.
Include $3.95 for shipping.
Please try your bookstore first.
You may write for a free catalog.

In Europe, Schiffer books are distributed by
Bushwood Books
6 Marksbury Ave.
Kew Gardens
Surrey TW9 4JF England
Phone: 44 (0) 20 8392-8585; Fax: 44 (0) 20 8392-9876
E-mail: info@bushwoodbooks.co.uk
Website: www.bushwoodbooks.co.uk
Free postage in the U.K., Europe; air mail at cost.

Contents

A Brief History of the Early Years

Ocean City, New Jersey was founded in 1879 by five Methodist ministers—brothers Ezra, S. Wesley, and James Lake, plus William Burrell and William Woods—along with the Lake brothers' father, Simon Lake.

The Lake brothers and Burrell sailed to the island known as Peck's Beach on September 10, 1879 in search of land where they could build a Christian seaside resort in which to hold their summer campground meetings. The eight-mile-long island, bounded by the Atlantic Ocean on the east and the Great Egg Harbor Bay on the west, and with only one permanent resident, was perfect. They planned to buy all of the land, survey the lots, deed restrict each lot to prevent the manufacture or sale of alcohol or the use of any building for prostitution or gambling, and suppress business and recreation on Sunday by ordinance. They would then sell the lots and begin the process of creating a year-round community to support the summer resort.

The Lakes and Burrell took their vision back to Simon Lake, father of the Lake brothers and a prosperous farmer and state legislator, and to William Woods, another Methodist minister. In October 1879, Simon Lake agreed to mortgage his farm to finance the project. By November of that year, they had decided to call the island Ocean City and the association that would govern it, the Ocean City Association, and had begun the process of surveying the land, laying out streets, and issuing stock.

Although undoubtedly motivated by the desire to build a Christian resort governed by their strong religious beliefs, the men were also very astute businessmen and realized the necessity of building a strong year-round community if the resort was to be successful.

Within a few months, after setting aside land for the Tabernacle, the Ocean City Association Office, and the Camp Meeting, they began selling lots and building houses, hotels, and buildings suitable for various businesses. They opened a school in the association office and encouraged others to open businesses. A newspaper, the *Ocean City Sentinel*, was started.

The Association, with William Wood as president and William Burrell as vice president, organized the Pleasantville and Ocean City Railroad Company to bring a train from Pleasantville, New Jersey to Somers Point, across the bay from Ocean City. They bought a steamboat to ferry passengers to the island.

The Association also opened the First National Bank of Ocean City and the Ocean City Title and Trust Company. S. Wesley Lake was director of both. Brother Ezra organized an electric light company, plus water and sewer companies. By 1881, a United States Post Office opened in Ocean City with William Burrell appointed postmaster. This was a great accomplishment, because it meant that the federal government recognized Ocean City as a legal entity.

By 1884, the town had grown so much that the majority of Association members felt they could no longer manage its business, religious, and political affairs, so they decided to incorporate Ocean City as a borough, meaning that the Ocean City Association was no longer the governing body. A mayor and councilmen were elected. The city founders feared that with the change in governance would come the end of the Sunday ordinances the Association had strictly enforced. But, although these ordinances were relaxed as the years went by, it took another century before they were completely removed. In 1897, Ocean City was incorporated as a city.

Ocean City grew quickly as a year-round and summer community and by 1900, had 2,000 permanent residents, eight large hotels, and many smaller hotels and cottages for summer vacationers. The boardwalk, first built in 1887, was expanded in 1905 and a Music Pavilion was built on the boardwalk at that time.

Trains continued to bring visitors to Ocean City, and with a trolley bridge built in 1907 between Somers Point and Ocean City, a ferry ride was no longer required to get to town. Ferry service ended completely in 1918.

As the use of automobiles became common, two auto bridges to Ocean City were built: one from Somers Point and one from Upper Township, farther south. Both bridges were officially opened in 1914.

As the year-round population and the popularity of the city as a summer resort continued to grow, so did the building of hotels, theaters, restaurants, and businesses. All of that was halted on the evening of October 11, 1927, however, when a fire destroyed a large portion of the boardwalk and then rolled up the main street, devastating everything in its path. By the time the fire was over, $3 million in damage had been done and several of the large hotels plus many homes and businesses were gone. By June of the following summer, a new, larger boardwalk had been completed and the restoration of hotels and homes was well underway.

The Depression slowed, but did not stop, the city's growth, and after World War II, Ocean City experienced a real building boom, much like other parts of the country.

On September 14, 1944, the largest hurricane of the century hit Ocean City, causing an estimated $2 million in damages. More than fifty homes were completely destroyed and many more badly damaged. In many places on the island, the ocean and bay actually met, and for several days after the storm it was impossible to get in or out of town or access some areas of the city during high tide. Large sections of the boardwalk were washed away and the rest was badly damaged. When the boardwalk was rebuilt, it was shorter by several blocks, as the most northerly part was not replaced.

Fortunately, the storm hit after most of the summer residents had left, and the city had nine months in which to rebuild. By June of 1945, Ocean City was ready for its usual influx of vacationers.

When the War ended on August 14, Ocean City, like the rest of the country, celebrated with joy! President Truman proclaimed a two-day national holiday and almost everything in town closed. Only the lifeguards, police, and firemen remained on duty.

In 1954, Ocean City celebrated its seventy-fifth anniversary with a yearlong celebration of the city's diamond jubilee. All over town, a mermaid holding a scallop shell and a diamond appeared on advertisements, signs, and memorabilia.

Postcards have always been a delightful way to document places and events, and here they are used to recount the first seventy-five years of Ocean City's history. Enjoy!

Nine views of local attractions are crowded onto this postcard.

This postcard says it all!

Postcards were a popular way to document vacations to Ocean City.

This view of the beach and boardwalk looking towards 9th Street was taken during the early 1930s.

Summer fun in Ocean City, NJ.

7

"Greetings from Ocean City, N.J."

Each of the letters on this postcard shows a different view while spelling out Ocean City.

Another postcard with each of the letters showing different attractions.

On the Strand

"Greetings from Ocean City, New Jersey."

In 1909, beach attire allowed for little sun bathing.

The Lock Step on the Beach

At Oce..... City, N. J.

80-5

View of Beach - Ocean City, N. J.

In the early part of the twentieth century, people went down to the beach in their Sunday best!

"Quiet Water," quiet enjoyment.

The Tahoma Restaurant, at 8th Street and the board-walk, was a popular spot for Sunday lunch in 1905.

QUIET WATER, OCEAN CITY, N.J.

Boardwalk and Beach, looking North from 8th St.
Ocean City, N.J.

Women went down to the strand in their
"summer whites" in the early 1900s.

The Beach at the Bathing Hour, Ocean City, N. J.

The beach at 9th Street, looking towards the Music Pavilion, was almost deserted before the summer season began.

Bathers used Shriver's boardwalk pavilion to get out of the sun.

Beach and Boardwalk, Ocean City, N. J.

SHRIVER'S BATHS

Bird's-Eye View of Beach Front, Ocean City, N. J.

SEASIDE BATHS.

Seaside Baths, opened in 1917, was one of the first stops for people visiting the beach for the day.

The Beach between 9th & 10th St.,
Ocean City, N. J.

Most of the bathers were men in 1906. The lifeguards' first aid tent is in the middle of this picture, which shows the beach between 9th and 10th Streets.

The "Sindia" wrecked Dec. 15, 1901, Ocean City, N. J.

A four-masted ship, the *Sindia*, came ashore between 16th and 17th Streets on December 15, 1901.

On October 8, 1911, a 58-foot long whale washed ashore at 4th Street.

Huge Whale Washed Ashore.
(Photo. by H. B. Smith.)

Ocean City, N. J.

218890

HOSPITAL TENT. OCEAN CITY. N. J.

This 1925 postcard shows the beach patrol first aid station at 10th Street.

The 1926 lifeguards lined up in front of their beach patrol head-quarters at 10th Street. Captain Jack Jernee is on the far right. The Flanders Hotel towers over the beach.

Daily Dozen at 32nd St., Ocean City, N. J.

CH PATROL, OCEAN CITY, N. J.

123779

W. Ward Beam leads a group of women in beach exercises on the 32nd Street beach in 1925.

The Daily Dozen Health Exercises on the Beach, Ocean City, N. J.

Boardwalk and Beach at 4th St., Ocean City, N. J.

"The Daily Dozen Health Exercises on the Beach."

Beachgoers at 4th Street stop for a photograph in the late 1920s.

111:—6th Street Bathing Beach, Ocean City, N. J.

The 6th Street beach was crowded in 1930.

General View of Beach at 4th Street, Ocean City, N. J.

The 4th Street lifeguard headquarters (on left surrounded by flags) made the beach a popular one.

GENERAL BEACH SCENE AT 2ND STREET LOOKING NORTH, OCEAN CITY, N. J.   29

The 2nd Street beach was a sea of beach umbrellas in 1934.

The Beach Patrol, Ocean City, N. J.

This view of Ocean City Beach Patrol lifeguards lined up with their boats for an intra-squad rowing race was a popular postcard in the 1930s.

These Ocean City lifeguards have their boats ready for a 1931 intra-squad doubles rowing race championship.

139:—OCEAN CITY LIFE GUARD BOAT CREWS. OCEAN CITY, N. J.

46051

On the Beach at Park Place, Ocean City, N. J.

This view of the beach at 4th Street shows the lifeguard headquarters, which was washed away during a storm in 1932.

"The Anglers Club Pier at Park Place."

The Anglers Club Fishing Pier, seen behind the lifeguards and their boat, was washed away in the same 1932 storm that destroyed the 4th Street lifeguard headquarters.

WATCHING THE NATIONAL LIFE GUARD TOURNAMENT, OCEAN CITY, N. J. 3

The local beach patrol hosted the National Lifeguard Tournament in 1934. They won for the second year in a row.

100:—Aeroplane View of Beach and Boardwalk, Ocean City, N. J.

This aerial view of 10th Street shows the huge crowd lined up to watch the National Lifeguard Tournament.

The 1934 National Lifeguard Tournament was held in front of the beach patrol headquarters at 10th Street.

EMERGENCY HOSPITAL ON THE BEACH AT 10TH STREET, OCEAN CITY, N. J.

2

BEACH SCENE AT FISHING PIER, OCEAN CITY, N. J.

49561

The 14th Street fishing pier was a private fishing club.

The fishing pier at 59th Street was a public fishing pier.

59th Street Bathing Beach and Public Fishing Pier, Ocean City, N. J.

1B-H1892

A Good Catch at Ocean City, N. J.

R. M. Jereissati, Ocean City, N. J.

These children look in awe at the one that **didn't** get away!

62

The Rock Jetty and Fishing Pier at 59th Street, Ocean City, N. J.

66600

These women are standing on the rock jetty near the 59th Street fishing pier.

A Happy Crowd on the Beach, Ocean City, N. J.

2+820

"A Happy Crowd on the Beach."

"EXERCISES" ON THE BEACH, OCEAN CITY, N. J.

Elmer E. Unger took over the beach exercise classes from W. Ward Beam in 1930. Classes were held on the 2nd Street beach Monday, Wednesday, and Friday at 11a.m.

THE BEACH CLASS AT 12TH STREET, OCEAN CITY, N. J.

Elmer Unger led his beach classes at 12th Street on Tuesdays, Thursdays, and Saturdays.

Because of the need for more bather protection in the growing north end, this beach patrol headquarters was built in 1938 at 1st Street.

206:-BEACH SCENE AT 2ND STREET, OCEAN CITY, N. J.

47359

151:—BEACH SCENE AT 14TH STREET, OCEAN CITY, N. J

The 14th Street beach always drew a crowd.

The lifeguard first aid station at 14th Street.

200:-BEACH SCENE AT 2ND STREET, OCEAN CITY, N. J.

47353

The beach umbrella concession was very busy on the 2nd Street beach.

13th Street Beach, Ocean City, N. J.

8A-H2249

From the back: "Ocean City's gently sloping bathing beaches of clean, soft sand are one of the most outstanding attractions to the multitudes of visitors who throng this popular resort."

Bird's Eye View of Beach Front — looking North — Ocean City, N. J.

2

This "Bird's Eye View" of the beachfront looks north from 15th Street towards Atlantic City.

The New Beachfront at Ocean City, N.J.

K6359

In April 1952, a state-city pumping project started. By the Fourth of July, the beach from 13th Street to the north end of the island was wide and ready for visitors.

The beach is the background for fun activities.

OCEAN CITY

NEW JERSEY

K7836

606

The Boardwalk

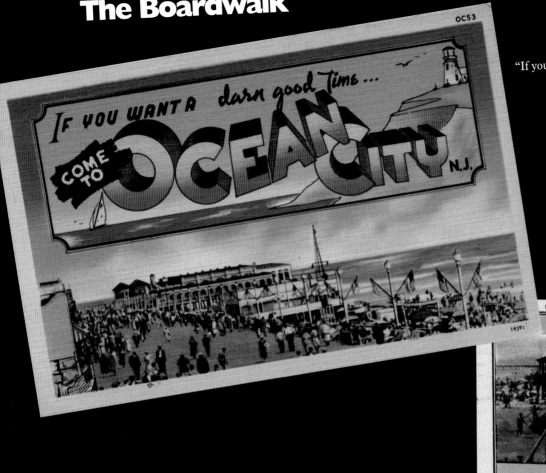

"If you want a darn good time…come to Ocean City, N.J."

Boardwalk fun is shown on this "Greetings" card.

BOARDWALK AT 11TH STREET   THE FLANDERS

GREETINGS FROM
OCEAN CITY, N.J.

ANGLER'S CLUB PIER, OCEAN CITY, N.J.   "SURF"

The Casino Pier, built in 1899 at 9th Street, was the first boardwalk pier. In 1904, it was purchased by John Lake Young and reopened as Young's Pier.

Young's Pier, Ocean City, N. J.

Hotel Lafayette Ocean Cy. N. Jersey

Boardwalk above Moorlyn Terrace, Ocean City, N. J.

638-4

On April 22, 1905, Mayor Joseph G. Champion dedicated the new, two-mile long boardwalk.

The Municipal Pier, known as the Music
Pavilion, was completed in 1905 and located
on the boardwalk at Moorlyn Terrace.

PUBLIC MUSIC PAVILION & PIER, OCEAN CITY, N. J.

DOUGHTY'S PIER, OCEAN CITY, N. J.

Doughty's Pier was at 8th Street.

Boardwalk above Tenth Street, Ocean City, N. J.

Shriver's opened in 1898. Its pavilion was across the boardwalk and afforded a place to rest.

Boardwalk below Seventh Street, Ocean City, N. J.

The boardwalk was a busy place in the early 1900s.

Easter Crowd on the Boardwalk, Ocean City, N. J.

"Easter Crowd on the Boardwalk." The Music Pavilion is on the left.

The original Casino Pier (later Young's Pier) was enlarged until, as the Hippodrome Pier, it extended far over the ocean. It was the resort's largest and most popular amusement center.

A Holiday Crowd on Boardwalk, Looking South towards Hippodrome, Ocean City, N. J.

Beach and Boardwalk at 10th St., Ocean City, N. J.

Day trippers had a choice of several bath houses on the boardwalk, where "sterilized suits and towels" could be rented by the day.

This early 1920s picture was taken from the pier at 9th Street looking south.

BIRD'S-EYE VIEW FROM OCEAN PIER, OCEAN CITY, N. J.

The Faunce Theatre was on the boardwalk at 10th Street.

SCENE ON THE

N. J.

Boardwalk Looking South from Hippodrome, Ocean City, N. J.

The Hippodrome Pier advertised that it had a "splendid auditorium seating 2,800 people."

This crowd on the boardwalk was typical on weekends.

Crowd on the Boardwalk, Ccean City, N. J.

Boardwalk Looking South from Doughty's Pier, Ocean City, N. J.

"Boardwalk Looking South from Doughty's Pier, Ocean City, N.J."

BOARDWALK, SHOWING BABY PARADE, OCEAN CITY, N. J.

The first Baby Parade was held in 1901.

The Baby Parade always drew a crowd.

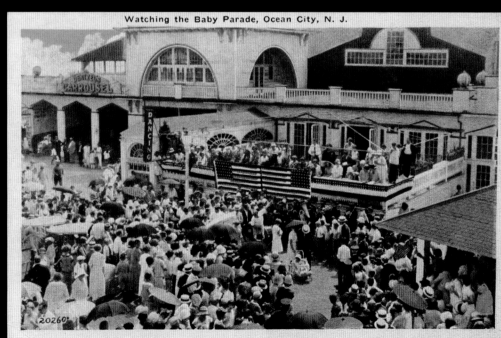

Watching the Baby Parade, Ocean City, N. J.

20260

Steeplechase Pier and Boardwalk, Ocean City, N. J.

The Steeplechase Pier was a popular amusement center.

Board Walk looking South from 8th Street, Ocean City, N. J.

Rolling chairs were always in demand on the boardwalk.

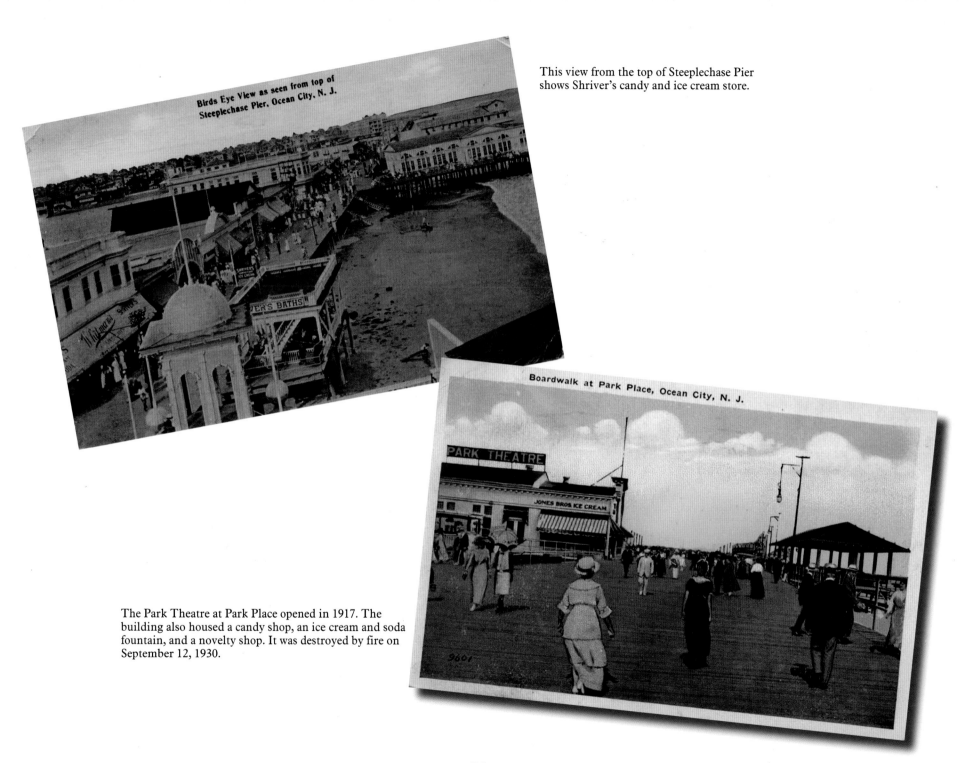

This view from the top of Steeplechase Pier shows Shriver's candy and ice cream store.

The Park Theatre at Park Place opened in 1917. The building also housed a candy shop, an ice cream and soda fountain, and a novelty shop. It was destroyed by fire on September 12, 1930.

General Boardwalk View South from 8th Street, Ocean City, N. J.

In 1940, the Ocean City Rotary Club met on Fridays at the Sheppard & Finsel Restaurant on 8th Street and the boardwalk.

The Moorlyn Theatre was across from the Music Pier.

Boardwalk, Front of Music Pier, Ocean City, N. J.

Strolling on the boardwalk was a good way to spend an afternoon.

8TH STREET AND BOARDWALK LOOKING SOUTH, OCEAN CITY, N. J.

Boardwalk View from 9th Street, Ocean City, N. J.

Window shopping on the boardwalk or going to the Strand Theatre at 9th Street were also pleasant afternoon activities.

66599

Boardwalk pavilions were good places to rest and watch the boardwalk strollers.

Shriver's Pavilion was always crowded.

Ryan's Restaurant was at 938 Boardwalk.

BOARDWALK, SOUTH FROM 10TH STREET, OCEAN CITY, N. J.

RYAN'S

— Try Ryan's Special 65¢ Dinner —

RYAN'S RESTAURANT, Ocean City, New Jersey — Open Day and Night

"Try Ryan's Special 65¢ Dinner – Ryan's Restaurant – Open Day and Night."

The boardwalk was rebuilt on a concrete base after the 1927 fire.

GENERAL VIEW BOARDWALK AND BEACH, OCEAN CITY, N. J.

RYAN'S

General View Beach and Boardwalk, Ocean City, N. J.   227

19581

Ocean City's was the first concrete-based boardwalk in the world.

BOARDWALK AT 6TH ST., OCEAN CITY, N. J.

The Playland carousel and Convention Hall can be seen in this view at 6th Street.

Bird's Eye View of Beachfront in the Gardens, Ocean City, N. J.

K6363

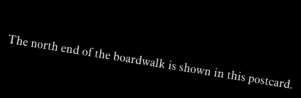

The north end of the boardwalk is shown in this postcard.

From the back: " In Ocean City you will meet the friendly, worthwhile people of your own social and business set, relaxing in carefree mood and enjoying the endless variety of amusements and entertainment offered the visitors."

Beach Front from the Air, Ocean City, N. J.

8A-H2247

224 Boardwalk and Concert Hall, Ocean City, N. J.

17,171

Beach cover-ups were required when walking the boardwalk in bathing attire—three of these women could have been arrested!

Boardwalk View Looking North, Ocean City, N. J.

K6599

People strolled the boardwalk in the afternoons and early evenings.

Boardwalk parades always had lots of spectators.

Boardwalk Parade, Ocean City, N. J.

SHRIVER'S

K 1306

MOONLIGHT VIEW BOARDWALK, NORTH FROM 12TH STREET, OCEAN CITY, N. J.   OC60

The Golden Galleon Building, between 11th and 12th Streets, was Ocean City's most exclusive shopping center.

The boardwalk shops stayed open in the evenings.

Boardwalk at Music Pier at Night, Ocean City, N. J.

"AMERICA'S GREATEST FAMILY RESORT"

Simms' SEAFOOD RESTAURANT — BOARDWALK — OCEAN CITY, NEW JERSEY

From the back: "Simms' Seafood Restaurant, Ocean City's leading restaurant since 1912. Located on the famous Boardwalk overlooking the Atlantic Ocean and having a seating capacity of 400. The spacious Simms' parking area, adjacent to the restaurant, is free to restaurant patrons."

Daily Flag Raising, Boardwalk, Moorlyn Terrace, Ocean City, N. J.

OB-H1893

FLAG RAISING CEREMONY AT MUSIC HALL ON THE BOARDWALK, OCEAN CITY, N. J.

E-4660

At 9:30 every morning, Captain Jack Jernee led his lifeguards in the raising and salute to the flag.

The daily flag raising ceremony began on July 4, 1940 and was continued every summer until the end of World War II. The scene was popularized on many Ocean City postcards from the 1940s.

Music Pier and Bathing Beach, Ocean City, N. J.

The Music Pier was built in 1928 at Moorlyn Terrace. The lookout tower was added after the attack on Pearl Harbor and was manned 24 hours a day to watch for enemy aircraft.

ncert in Music Hall, 8th and Boardwalk, Ocean City, N. J.

The Music Pier held free daily concerts throughout the summer.

City Views, City Scenes

This postcard shows some of the important buildings in 1940s Ocean City.

The U.S. Lifesaving Station at 4th Street and Atlantic Avenue.

3601 Central Avenue, Ocean City, N. J.
Summer Program for Boys — 10-18 years of age

Ocean City (Naval Training) Academy

The Ocean City (Naval Training) Academy was formerly the 36th Street U.S. Lifesaving Station. Former Beach Patrol Captain Jack Jernee opened the Academy in 1946.

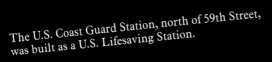

The U.S. Coast Guard Station, north of 59th Street, was built as a U.S. Lifesaving Station.

391.   U. S. COAST GUARD STATION, NORTH OF 59TH STREET.   OCEAN CITY, N. J.

The house on the left was the home of Rev. William Burrell, and the one on the right the home of Rev. Ezra B. Lake. Both were founders of Ocean City.

View from the Park, Ocean City, N. J.

OCEAN CITY VOLUNTEER FIRE CO., OCEAN CITY, N.J.
5762

In 1896, the City's first firehouse was built on 9th Street near Asbury Avenue. The bell in the tower was rung to call the firemen to duty.

This is Ocean City's original steam fire engine. It is a horse-drawn 1902 Silsby Steamer. This engine was well adapted for seashore fire fighting because if no fresh water was available, bay water could be used.

Asbury Ave. looking North from Eighth St., Ocean City, N. J.

A view of Asbury Avenue looking north from 8th Street before the automobile age.

WEST FROM NINTH STREET, OCEAN CITY, N. J.

NORTH FROM NINTH STREET, OCEAN CITY, N. J.

Intersection of 9th Street and Wesley Avenue. The green-roofed building on the right is the Strand Hotel and the light green building on the left is the Traymore Hotel.

Looking north from 9th Street.

WESLEY AVENUE, NORTH OF NINTH ST. OCEAN CITY, N. J.

The electric trolley began operating in 1893, running from 1st Street to 17th Street. By 1898, it had been extended to 59th Street.

This view of 8th Street and Wesley Avenue shows the trolley in the distance.

WESLEY AVENUE LOOKING WEST, OCEAN CITY, N. J.

Wesley Avenue above 10th Street, Ocean City, N. J.

"Wesley Avenue above 10th Street."

Central Ave. looking North showing High School, Ocean City, N. J.

"Central Avenue looking North showing High School."

8th Street looking West Showing Hotel Mayberry, Ocean City, N. J.

"8th Street looking west showing Hotel Mayberry" (on the left corner).

BOARD WALK AT MOORLYN TERRACE, OCEAN CITY, N. J.

New Jersey Governor Woodrow Wilson spoke in the Hippodrome Building, on the boardwalk at Moorlyn Terrace, on September 28, 1911.

The Massey and Edwards Building on the corner of 8th Street and Central Avenue was used by the City Council until they moved into City Hall in 1915.

City Hall opened in 1915 on the corner of 9th Street and Asbury Avenue. The police and firemen also used the building.

8TH STREET, WEST FROM OCEAN AVENUE, OCEAN CITY, N. J.

The small building in the foreground is the J. W. Morrison Realtors office. The large building is the Biscayne Hotel.

Written on the back of this card: "How would you like to go to this school? With love, Aunt Grace." Postmarked May 7, 1908. The school opened in 1907 on Central Avenue between 8th and 9th Streets.

HIGH SCHOOL, OCEAN CITY, N. J.

The new Ocean City High School opened in 1924 on Atlantic Avenue between 5th and 6th Streets. Townspeople were convinced that this was the best high school building in New Jersey.

OCEAN CITY HIGH SCHOOL, SIXTH AND ATLANTIC AVENUE, OCEAN CITY, N. J.

124:—THE OCEAN CITY HIGH SCHOOL, OCEAN CITY, N. J.

This view is of the back of the 1924 High School.

46050

Ocean City Title and Trust Bank, Asbury Ave.,

Ocean City, N. J.

24816

On May 29, 1925, the Ocean City Title and Trust Company moved into its new seven-story building on the corner of 8th Street and Asbury Avenue. It was the largest office building in Cape May County.

New First National Bank Bldg., 8th and Asbury Ave., Ocean City, N. J.

1901 FIRST NATIONAL BANK 1923

The First National Bank served the financial needs of the community beginning in 1901.

Asbury Ave. Looking South from 8th St., Ocean City, N. J.

Looking south from the corner of 8th Street and Asbury Avenue.

Asbury Ave., North from 8th St., Ocean City, N. J.

Looking north from the corner of 8th Street and Asbury Avenue.

20 ASBURY AVENUE NORTH FROM 9TH STREET, OCEAN CITY, N. J.   123781

City Hall is on the right in this picture.

ASBURY AVENUE LOOKING NORTH, OCEAN CITY, N. J.

The G. C. Murphy Company opened in 1929 in the Bourse Building on Asbury Avenue at 8th Street.

8th St. East of Asbury Ave., Ocean City, N. J.

Notice the Shore Fast Line Trolley in the center of the street. It ran from Atlantic City's boardwalk to Ocean City's boardwalk.

Post Office and Elberon Hotel, 8th Street, Ocean City, N. J.

The Ocean City Post Office was located in the building on the right from 1910 to 1937. The Elberon Hotel is on the left with the porch.

NEW POST OFFICE. 9TH STREET AND OCEAN AVENUE. OCEAN CITY, N. J.

10

It cost a penny to mail a postcard and three pennies to mail a letter when the U.S. Post Office moved into this building in 1937.

From the back: "Watson's Coffee Shop, Ocean Avenue at 9th Street. The Most Popular Restaurant in America's Greatest Family Resort."

Johnson's Ice Cream and Candy Shop at 4th Street opened in 1930. It was famous for its ice cream cones—a sour candy ball was dropped into the bottom of each one.

BOARDWALK AT 4TH STREET BY MOONLIGHT. OCEAN CITY. N. J.

OC 73

Coffee Shop, Cor. 8th and Wesley Ave., Ocean City, N. J.

The Marlyn Coffee Shop advertised, "Make Marlyn a Habit...It's a Good One!"

From the back: "The Chatterbox...the Popular Spot to Meet and Eat in Ocean City."

Florida Inn Restaurant, Ocean City, N. J.

The Florida Inn, between Wesley and Ocean Avenues on 8th Street. From the back: "Good Food...Moderate Prices...Friendly Atmosphere."

The Stanton Restaurant, on 9th Street near the boardwalk, advertised: "When quality is desired, visit our healthful air-conditioned dining room."

The Ocean City Home Savings and Loan Association invited the public to tour its new building at 10th Street and Asbury Avenue when it opened on August 16, 1950. The banking institution traces its roots back to 1887 and the Ocean City Building and Loan Association.

The City founders kept the land between 5th and 6th
Streets from the bay to the ocean for public use.

BEAUTIFUL RESIDENTIAL STREET IN OCEAN CITY, NEW JERSEY

OC 74

World War Memorial, Ocean City, N. J.

Looking north from 12th Street along Wesley Avenue.

On May 27, 1947, the World War I Monument and
the World War II Honor Roll were moved from
the City Hall lawn to the park between 5th and 6th
Streets on Wesley Avenue.

72

Where We Played

"Greetings from Ocean City N.J. / America's Greatest Family Resort."

This "Greetings from Ocean City" card shows the golf course, Hotel Flanders swimming pool, and the beaches.

"Down she goes"   AT OCEAN CITY. N, J.

"A Good Day's Catch."

Across from the Music Pavilion, the Moore Building was a center of attraction with its bowling casino.

The bowling casino had ten bowling lanes.

Casino Bowling Alleys, Ocean City, N. J.

General View of Boardwalk at 6th St., Ocean City, N. J.

Playland, a $100,000 amusement center, opened at 6th Street and the boardwalk in 1930. It housed a merry-go-round and one of the largest and most modern penny arcades on the Jersey Coast.

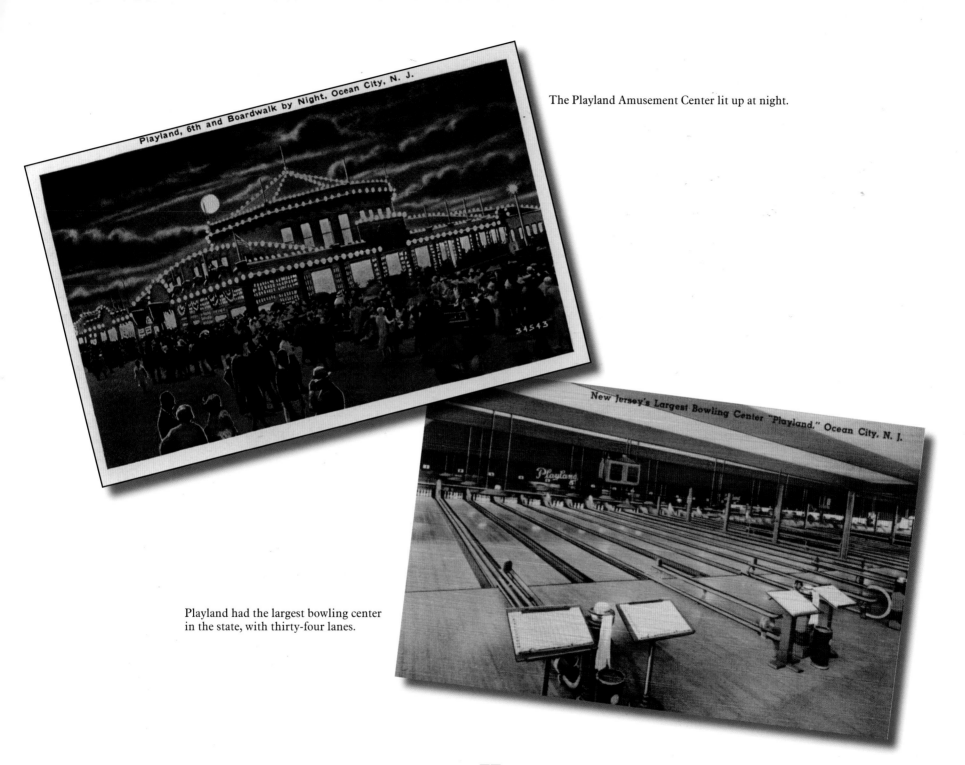

The Playland Amusement Center lit up at night.

Playland had the largest bowling center
in the state, with thirty-four lanes.

Playland opened the largest roller skating rink in South Jersey in 1939.

The Ocean City Golf Club opened in 1927. One of the finest courses along the coast, it was open all year to both men and women golfers.

226   The "Fun Deck" Plymouth Place and Boardwalk, Ocean City, N. J.

17,173

In 1930, the Ferris Wheel was the main attraction at Gillian's Fun Deck, Plymouth Place and the boardwalk.

The Ferris Wheel from Gillian's Fun Deck could be seen from the boardwalk.

General Boardwalk View, Ocean City, N. J.

K6357

With thirty courts, Ocean City advertised that it had the largest shuffleboard center north of St. Petersburg, Florida. The courts were open 9 a.m. to 10:30 p.m.

Ocean City boasted twenty-two of the finest clay tennis courts in New Jersey.

Sailing on the Great Egg Harbor Bay was a favorite pastime.

The Hydrangea Trail went from Atlantic City south through Ocean City to Wildwood Crest.

The first swimming pool at Hotel Flanders opened on May 30, 1924. The pool drew hundreds of visitors each day, and large crowds attended the aquatic shows put on by members of the Ocean City Beach Patrol.

In 1929, The Flanders opened three more swimming pools. The large pool, the diving pool, and the children's pool can be seen in this aerial view.

Bicycle riding on Ocean City's two-and-one-half-mile-long boardwalk was a favorite pastime for residents and visitors.

Where We Stayed

FOUR GOOD REASONS WHY YOU SHOULD COME TO OCEAN CITY N.J.

"Four Good Reasons Why You Should Come to Ocean City, N.J. / The Flanders Hotel / Safe and Wide Beach / Wide Boardwalk / Sailing, Fishing and Other Sports."

The Brighton Hotel was built in 1880 on the corner of 7th Street and Ocean Avenue. When it was built, it was so close to the beach that ocean spray frequently showered its wide verandas.

This was a commonly seen postcard in the 1930s. On the back is printed, "The Brighton, Ocean City's Premier Hotel." The hotel was torn down in 1940.

The Traymore Hotel was on the corner of 9th Street and Wesley Avenue. When it was built in the 1890s, it had grounds for croquet and lawn tennis. The Ocean City Electric Trolley ran down Wesley Avenue. The Traymore was destroyed in the 1927 fire.

Normandie on the Sea, Ocean City, N. J.

9586

Originally built in the early 1890s as the Aetna, renamed the Cumberland, and then the Normandie on the Sea, this hotel stood on the corner of 9th Street and Ocean Avenue. It, too, was destroyed in the fire of 1927.

Mayberry, Ocean City, N. J.

The Mayberry Hotel was located at 8th Street and Wesley Avenue.

Wesley Arms Hotel — 801 Wesley Ave., Ocean City, N. J.

The Wesley Arms Hotel was originally the Mayberry.

The Strand, on the corner of 9th Street and Wesley Avenue, was advertised in 1894 as having: "The Finest and Most Select Location. Rooms en Suite with Private Bath, Liberal Management, Music."

STRAND HOTEL. OCEAN CITY. N. J.

The Oceanic Hotel, on Wesley Avenue between 11th and 12th Streets, was open all year and had steam heat.

The Oceanic—Ocean City, N. J.

Westley Ave. looking South.
Showing Swarthmore Hotel, Ocean City, N. J.

"Wesley Avenue looking South, Showing Swarthmore Hotel."

HOTEL SWARTHMORE, OCEAN CITY, N.J.

The Swarthmore Hotel had unobstructed ocean views and over one hundred rooms. It was located on Wesley Avenue between 9th and 10th Streets.

The Atglen, Ocean City, N. J.

The Atglen Hotel was at 9th Street and Central Avenue. It had a capacity of seventy-five people and offered, "Special Rates."

The Fairview Hotel was on 8th Street between Ocean and Wesley Avenues.

FAIRVIEW HOTEL, OCEAN CITY, N. J.

BISCAYNE HOTEL, OCEAN CITY, N. J.

When New Jersey Governor Woodrow Wilson came to Ocean City he stayed at the Biscayne Hotel, 812 Ocean Avenue.

The Hotel Bellevue, Ocean City, N. J.

THE ILLINOIS, 926 WESLEY AVENUE, OCEAN CITY, N. J.

HOTEL LINCOLN, OCEAN CITY, NEW JERSEY

LINCOLN RESTAURANT

The Hotel Bellevue, on the corner of 8th Street and Ocean Avenue, advertised on the back of the postcard: "Modern Artistic Appointments, Superb Bathing Facilities, Health-giving, Absolutely Pure Drinking Water, Moderate Prices."

From the back: "The Illinois Hotel, 926 Wesley Avenue. One of Ocean City's Very Best, Centrally Located Hotels."

The Lincoln Hotel, at 9th Street and Wesley Avenue, was originally two hotels, The Waverly and The Hewlings. They were joined after World War I.

88

From the back: "The Colonial Hotel, on the Beach Front. Convenient to all Restaurants and Stores. No streets to cross to Boardwalk and Beach. All outside rooms and Florida type apts."

Colonial Hotel
831 Atlantic Ave.,
Ocean City, N. J.

COLONIAL

THE BREAKERS, OCEAN CITY, N. J.

The Breakers Hotel, on the boardwalk at Delancey Place, opened in 1912 as the first hotel on the boardwalk.

HOTEL DELAWARE, BOARDWALK AND 3rd ST., OCEAN CITY, N. J.

DELAWARE   HOTEL   DELAWARE

Hotel Delaware was built in 1925 on the boardwalk from 3rd Street to Park Place. Its advertisements boasted that all of its 175 rooms were fireproof.

This view from 8th Street and Ocean Avenue shows the Sterling Hotel.

EIGHTH & OCEAN AVES., SHOWING STERLING HOTEL, OCEAN CITY, N. J.

THE NEW HOTEL LA MONTE, OCEAN AVENUE AT 8TH STREET, OCEAN CITY, N. J.

The Sterling Hotel was joined with the St. Charles Hotel next door and reopened as the Hotel La Monte. From the back: "Sixty rooms with running water and several bath rooms on each sleeping floor. Large lobby, dining room, kitchen. Everything that any first-class hotel should have."

Steamer Landing and Hotel Comfort, 2nd and Bay Ave., Ocean City, N. J.

From the back: "Hotel Comfort, 210 Bay Avenue, situated at edge of the beautiful bay, and five minutes walk to the ocean and boardwalk."

HOTEL SOUTHERN, 835 FIFTH ST., OCEAN CITY, N. J.

Hotel Southern, at 835 5th Street, overlooked the city park. It was open May through September on the European plan.

From the back: "Croft Hall, 601 Atlantic Avenue, pleasant, cool rooms, hot and cold running water, comfortable beds."

CROFT HALL, 601 ATLANTIC AVENUE, OCEAN CITY, NEW JERSEY

GUESTS

OCEAN COURT APARTMENTS, OCEAN CITY, N. J.

THE BRIGHTON-ATLANTIC APTS., ATLANTIC AVE. AND BRIGHTON PLACE, OCEAN CITY, N. J.

The Ocean Court Apartments opened in 1927 at 3rd Street and Ocean Avenue. It was the first cooperative building.

The Brighton-Atlantic Apartments, Atlantic Avenue and Brighton Place, were (from the back), "Fire-proof and Sound-proof with Hardwood Flooring throughout, Hot Water at all times, and Concealed Radiation."

From the back: "Hotel Flanders, 11th Street and the Boardwalk, built in 1923 at a cost of a million and a half dollars. Capacity over 200 rooms."

The Flanders had parking for two hundred cars.

The Hotel Flanders had an elegant dining room, which served three meals a day, as well as rooms for special banquets.

The swimming pool at the Flanders was built between the Hotel's solariums in 1923.

Hotel Flanders Pool, Ocean City, N. J.

24805

HOTEL FLANDERS AND OUTDOOR SWIMMING POOLS, OCEAN CITY, N. J.

E-4681

In 1929, the Flanders opened three pools, and the era of the Ocean City Beach Patrol's gigantic water shows began.

THE HANIF INN
ROOMS

916 WESLEY AVENUE   OCEAN CITY, N. J.

MRS. ADA HANIFIN, PROP.

Zenneth Manor
728 Atlantic Ave., Ocean City, N. J.

The Hanif Inn at 916 Wesley Avenue was owned and oper-
ated by Mrs. Ada Hanifin.

From the back: "The Manor, at Moorlyn Terrace and Atlantic Avenue. One block from Beach, Music Pier, Bus Terminal. European Plan Hotel. Bathing from House. Phone. Owner Management."

Hotel Hanscom, at 8th Street just off the boardwalk, opened in 1929 as "Ocean City's New Modern, Fireproof Hotel."

The Alvyn Hotel on Brighton Place between 4th and 5th Streets. From the back: "An Adventure in Delightful Living."

Sindia Apartments – 18th St. and Wesley Ave. -- on the Beachfront – Ocean City, N. J.

The Sindia Apartments opened in 1940 at 18th Street and Wesley Avenue with forty modern apartments. They were advertised for rent starting at $350.00 for the season.

SINDIA EFFICIENCY APTS., 18th AND BOARDWALK, OCEAN CITY, N. J.

The Sindia Efficiency Apartments were adjacent to the boardwalk at 18th Street.

HOTEL SCARBOROUGH. 720 OCEAN AVE.. OCEAN CITY. N. J.

Hotel Scarborough, 720 Ocean Avenue. From the back: "Sixty Rooms, Private Baths and Showers – All Rooms have Running Water. Centrally Located. European Plan."

The Seaview — 1011 Ocean Avenue
Ocean City, N. J.

SEAVIEW

"The Seaview – 1011 Ocean Avenue." From the back: "The pleasant, friendly atmosphere of the Seaview will appeal to you. Its modern community kitchen is equipped with individual units. Right off the beach – bathing from Hotel."

From the back: "The Georgian, 1120 Central Avenue. All outside rooms, spacious lobby and porches."

HALCYON HALL
1116 WESLEY AVE.
OCEAN CITY, N. J.

HARRISON OWNERSHIP
MANAGEMENT

The Halcyon Hotel was located at 1116 Wesley Avenue.

Where We Worshipped

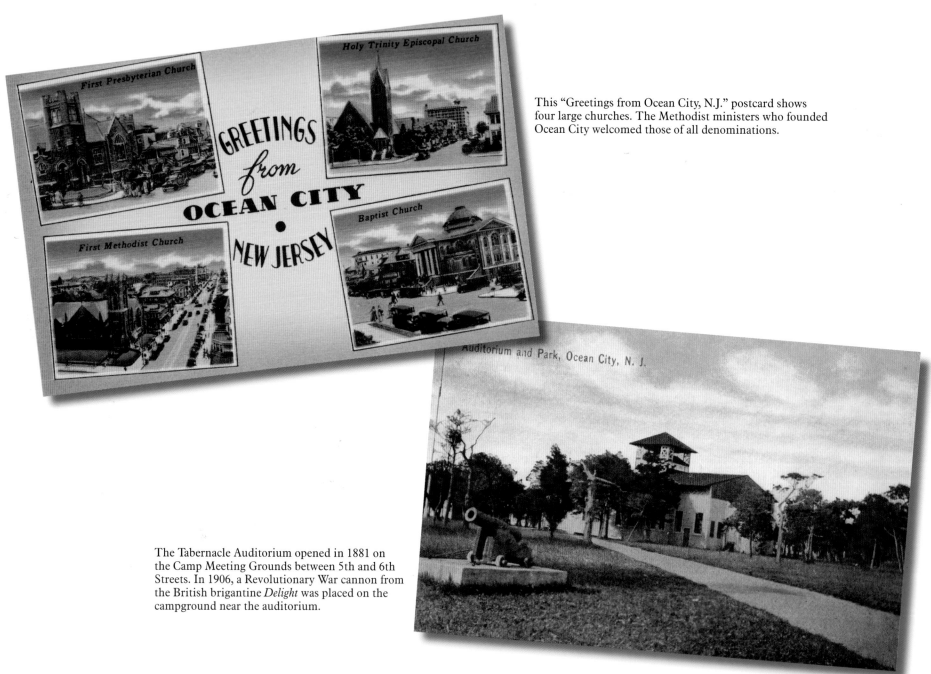

This "Greetings from Ocean City, N.J." postcard shows four large churches. The Methodist ministers who founded Ocean City welcomed those of all denominations.

The Tabernacle Auditorium opened in 1881 on the Camp Meeting Grounds between 5th and 6th Streets. In 1906, a Revolutionary War cannon from the British brigantine *Delight* was placed on the campground near the auditorium.

On the "Auditorium Square" can be seen the Tabernacle, right, and the Young People's Temple.

The Young People's Temple, built on the Auditorium grounds, opened on August 15, 1895.

The Women's Christian Temperance Union held many meetings on the Tabernacle Camp Grounds.

The Tabernacle Baptist Church, shown in this photo, is at 8th Street and West Avenue, where it was moved in 1907. It was built as the First Methodist Episcopal Church in 1890 at 8th Street and Central Avenue.

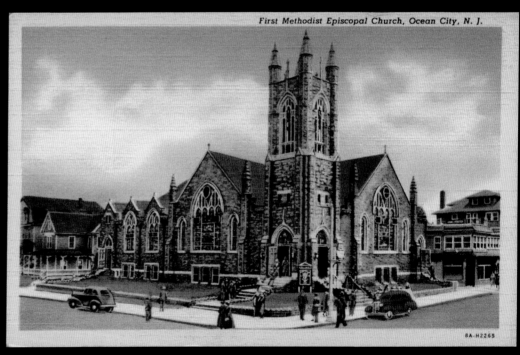

First Methodist Episcopal Church, Ocean City, N. J.

The new First Methodist Episcopal Church at 8th Street and Central Avenue was dedicated on July 4, 1909.

The Immanuel Baptist Church and Parsonage.

The Baptist Church was built in 1926 on the corner of 10th Street and Wesley Avenue.

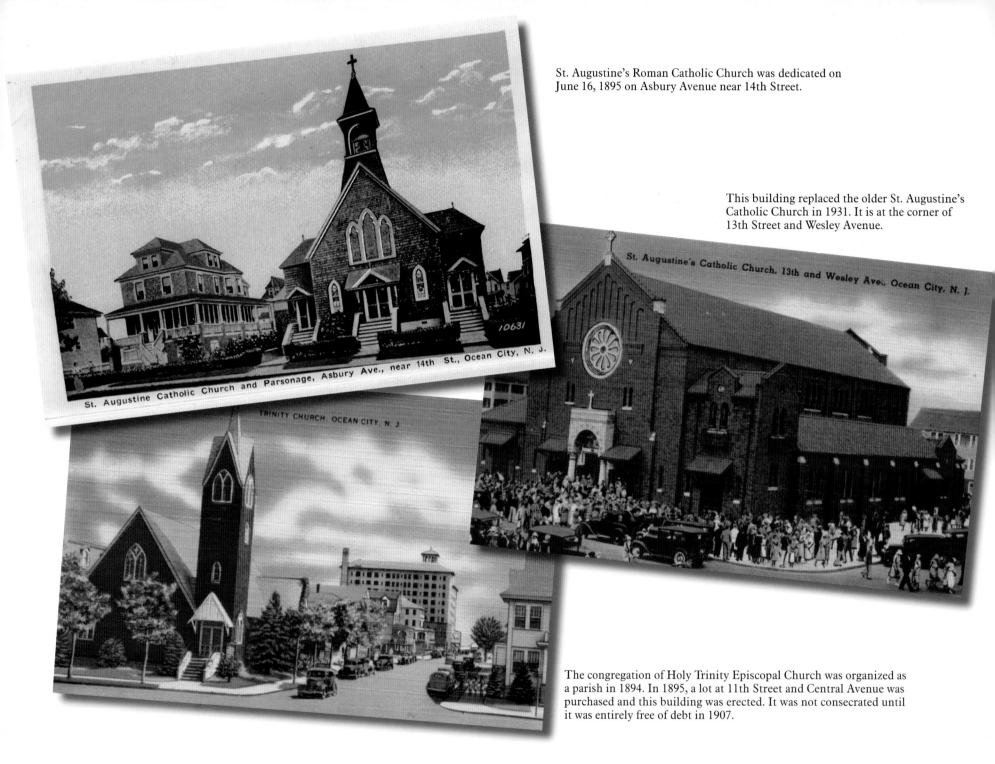

St. Augustine's Roman Catholic Church was dedicated on
June 16, 1895 on Asbury Avenue near 14th Street.

This building replaced the older St. Augustine's
Catholic Church in 1931. It is at the corner of
13th Street and Wesley Avenue.

The congregation of Holy Trinity Episcopal Church was organized as
a parish in 1894. In 1895, a lot at 11th Street and Central Avenue was
purchased and this building was erected. It was not consecrated until
it was entirely free of debt in 1907.

The Christian Brothers Summer School, Ocean Rest, at 31st Street and Central Avenue, opened in 1898.

"St. Mary's Church, 2nd and Atlantic Ave."

The First Presbyterian Church at 7th Street and Wesley Avenue held its first service in this building on March 27, 1907.

The Lutheran Church was built at 10th Street and Central Avenue in 1924.

"Greetings from New Jersey." Ocean City is on the map!

Ocean Drive, from the back: "Jersey Cape Scenic Route, 50 Glorious Miles within Sight and Sound of the Ocean."

"The Longport" Boat from Atlantic City for Ocean City, N. J.

The *Longport* steamer carried passengers between Atlantic City and Ocean City before the bridge to Somers Point was built at 9th Street.

The Steamer from Longport to Ocean City

The *Somers Point* steamer from Longport ferried passengers to Ocean City.

Beginning in 1897, the Philadelphia & Reading Railroad entered Ocean City at 52nd Street and went north on Haven Avenue, stopping at this depot on 10th Street.

PHILADELPHIA & READING R. R. DEPOT, OCEAN CITY, N. J.

BRIDGE APPROACHING OCEAN CITY

Scene along lines of Atlantic City & Shore Railroad, between Atlantic City and Ocean City

Trolley Service to Atlantic City
Eighth Street Terminal at Boardwalk, Oce...

STEEL PIER
VESSELLA'S
ITALIAN BAND

On July 2, 1907, the first electric trolley rolled across the new Somers Point-Ocean City trestle bridge, linking Ocean City to Somers Point, Linwood, Northfield, Pleasantville, and Atlantic City.

"Trolley Service to Atlantic City, 8th Street Terminal, Ocean City, N.J."

In 1914, the Ocean City Automobile Bridge Company opened the roadway and four bridges connecting Ocean City and Somers Point. In this view towards Ocean City, the automobile bridge can be seen beyond the trolley bridge.

ALL ROADS LEAD TO OCEAN CITY, N. J.

This 1920s postcard brags, "All Roads Lead to Ocean City."

"Aero View of Ocean City, N.J."

25 AERO VIEW OF OCEAN CITY, N. J.

171:—THE NEW OCEAN CITY—LONGPORT BRIDGE, OCEAN CITY, N. J.

The Ocean City-Longport Bridge opened in 1928.

Gardens Parkway approaching the Ocean City, Longport Bridge, Ocean City, N. J.

The Gardens Parkway in the north end of Ocean City is the approach to the Ocean City-Longport Bridge.

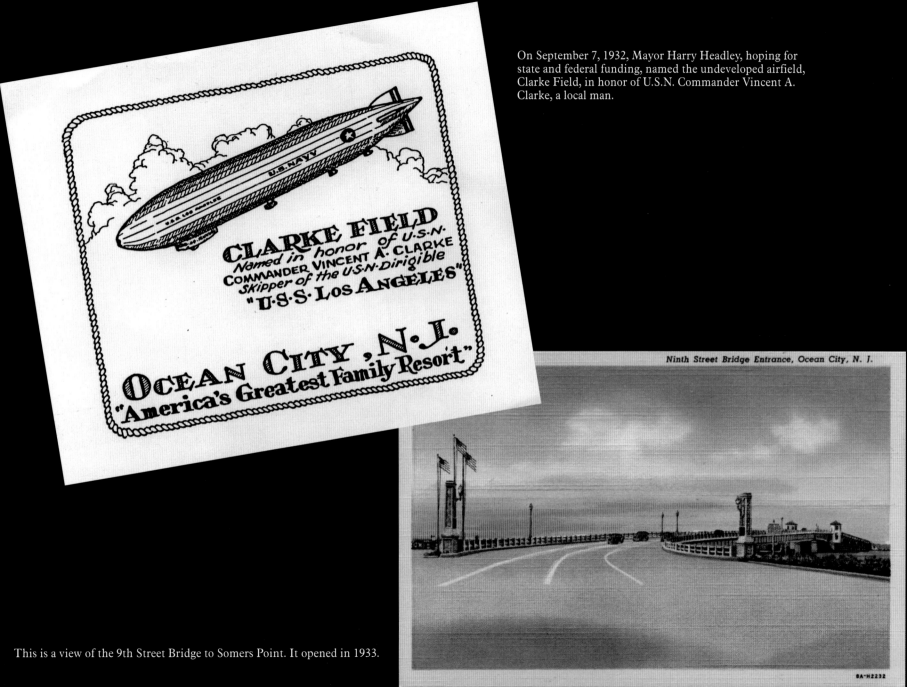

On September 7, 1932, Mayor Harry Headley, hoping for state and federal funding, named the undeveloped airfield, Clarke Field, in honor of U.S.N. Commander Vincent A. Clarke, a local man.

CLARKE FIELD
Named in honor of U.S.N.
COMMANDER VINCENT A. CLARKE
Skipper of the U.S.N. Dirigible
"U.S.S. Los Angeles"

OCEAN CITY, N.J.
"America's Greatest Family Resort"

Ninth Street Bridge Entrance, Ocean City, N. J.

This is a view of the 9th Street Bridge to Somers Point. It opened in 1933.

Edward G. Kurtz, Ocean City's first automobile dealer, began selling Ford cars in 1921. In 1941, from his dealership at 1st Street and Atlantic Avenue, he sent these postcards out as a promotion.

This promotional postcard was sent out by Palmer Chevrolet, 1119 Asbury Avenue, as encouragement to buy the 1953 Chevy Bel Air.

BIRD'S-EYE VIEW OF NEW MEMORIAL BRIDGE - OCEAN CITY TO SOMERS POINT, N. J.

13

E-4684

"Bird's-Eye View of New Memorial Bridge
– Ocean City to Somers Point.'

In 1953, these cars were backed up
at the drawbridge on the 9th Street
Bridge on their way out of town.

Toll Plaza on the Garden State Parkway of New Jersey.

When the Garden State Parkway opened in 1954, it was hailed as
a way for all of New Jersey to discover the Jersey Shore.

"Greetings from Ocean City." Sailing on the bay.

More fun on the bay and in the surf.

Ocean City Yacht Club, Ocean City, N. J.

The Ocean City Yacht Club at 6th Street and the bay was an excellent place to watch a boat parade.

The Carnival Night in Venice was a parade of decorated boats on the bay. The first Night in Venice was held on August 12, 1907.

Ready for the Carnival Night of Venice, Ocean City, N. J.

1908

New Yacht Club House, Ocean City, N. J.

The Ocean City Yacht Club formally opened their new clubhouse on August 24, 1912.

A seaplane landing in front of the Ocean City Yacht Club.

OCEAN CITY YACHT CLUB, OCEAN CITY, N. J.

Regatta at Ocean City Yacht Club on the Bay, Ocean City, N. J.

8A-H2233

The Ocean City Yacht Club began sponsoring speed boat races in the 1930s. The races were staged on Great Egg Harbor Bay.

"Bird's-Eye View of Lagoon," taken from the top of the Yacht Club.

BIRD'S-EYE VIEW OF LAGOON, OCEAN CITY, N. J.

The Pennsylvania Railroad and Y.M.C.A. Building was used by Pennsylvania railroad men who stayed there between runs to Philadelphia. Their families also used it as a vacation spot. The building was at the end of a pier and seemed to be surrounded by water.

Y. M. C. A. Boat Club, Ocean City, N. J.

Ocean City Motor Boat Club House, Ocean City, N. J.

The Ocean City Motor Boat Club House was at 15th Street and the bay. It opened in 1910.

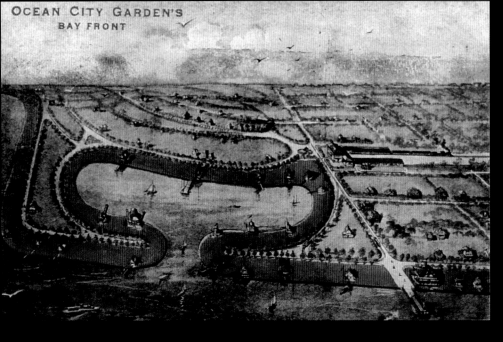

OCEAN CITY GARDEN'S
BAY FRONT

From the back of the postcard, postmarked 1910: "Beautiful Ocean City Gardens, Lots for Sale, High, Overlooking Ocean, All Streets Made, Cement Curbs and Sidewalks, Gas, Electricity, Sewers, Water and etc."

BAY FRONT VIEW, OCEAN CITY, N. J.

"Bay Front View."

From the back: "Yachting and boating enthusiasts can have endless pleasure and enjoy to the uttermost this exciting sport on the broad expanses of Great Egg Harbor Bay."

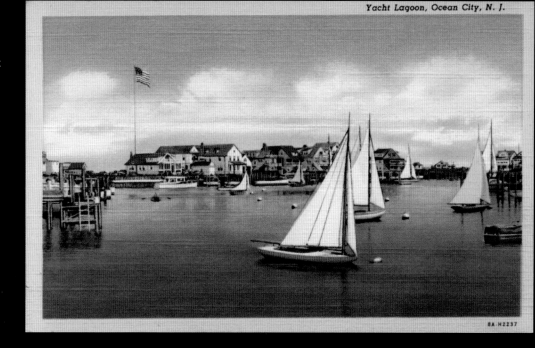

Yacht Lagoon, Ocean City, N. J.

8A-H2237

HARBOR SCENE   W114

14415

"Harbor Scene." The American flag is flying at the Coast Guard Station.

From the back: "Chris' Seafood Restaurant and Fish Market. All fish brought in daily by our own boats. We pack and ship, wholesale, to all parts of the country. No charge to see this daily catch."

SEAFOOD RESTAURANT

BECK'S SEA FOOD RESTAURANT AND MARKET.

OCEAN CITY, N. J.

"Beck's Sea Food Restaurant and Market." In 1939, the name was changed to Hogate's Restaurant. Beck's advertised that they served 47,759 patrons during the summer of 1936.

Hogate's Restaurant and Chris' Restaurant (to the right of Hogate's) could both be seen when coming over the 9th Street Bridge into Ocean City.

The 9th Street drawbridge can be seen in this bay front view looking north.

A 1948 aerial view of the 17th and 18th Streets Lagoons.

Air View of 17th and 18th Streets Lagoons, Ocean City, N. J.

K4947

This 550 foot long lagoon between 8th and 9th Streets was cut out in 1949.

The Ocean City Cruiser left from Chris' Dock at 9th Street on its daily eighteen mile bay and ocean cruise.

Ocean City Cruises - Chris' Dock - 9th St.

On the Bayfront - Ocean City, N. J.

Flying Saucer, Ocean City, N. J.

Chris Montagna, owner of Chris' Seafood Restaurant, owned a fleet of the finest and safest fishing boats and the fastest speedboats on the Atlantic coast. Sightseeing tours were given on the speedboats. The *Flying Saucer* was the most famous.

90831

"45 Minute Speedboat Ride on the Ocean at Ocean City." The *Flying Pony* was another of Chris' boats. It had a capacity of forty-five passengers and was powered by a 1400 H.P. motor.

The *Wild Goose* was a deep sea fishing boat and offered a thrilling ride on the ocean at 75 MPH each evening.

Two Hour Sailboat Ride on the Ocean at Ocean City, N.J.

CHRIS' RESTAURANT

91026

The *Sweetheart* sailed from Chris' Dock every morning and evening.

FLYING CLOUD, CHRIS' NEWEST FISHING BOAT, OCEAN CITY, N.J.

FLYING CLOUD   CHRIS RESTAURANT

E-14382

The *Flying Cloud* was a deep-sea fishing boat.

Gone with the Wind out of Chris' Dock.

"Gone with the Wind", Fishing Boat, Year around Fishing, Ocean City, N.J.

90763

Memorial Bridge, Ocean City to Somers Point, N. J.

OB-H1892

In this photo, the drawbridge at 9th Street is raised to allow a sailboat to pass through. Hogate's Restaurant advertised on this boat.

Beach and Bathing View, America's Greatest Family Resort, Ocean City, N. J.

K7842

In 1954, Ocean City celebrated its 75th Anniversary.

Bibliography

Miller, Fred. *Ocean City: America's Greatest Family Resort.* Charleston, South Carolina: Arcadia Publishing, 2003.

Miller, Fred. *Ocean City Beach Patrol.* Charleston, South Carolina: Arcadia Publishing, 2004.

Miller, Fred. *Ocean City: 1950-1980.* Charleston, South Carolina: Arcadia Publishing, 2006.